LIFE CYCLES

The Life Cycle of Mammals

Susan H. Gray

Chicago, Illinois

www.heinemannraintree.com
Visit our website to find out more information about Heinemann-Raintree books.

To order:

☎ Phone 888-454-2279

💻 Visit www.heinemannraintree.com to browse our catalog and order online.

© 2012 Heinemann Library
an imprint of Capstone Global Library, LLC
Chicago, Illinois

Edited by Abby Colich, Megan Cotugno, and Kate deVilliers
Designed by Victoria Allen
Illustrated by Darren Lingard
Picture research by Hannah Taylor
Originated by Capstone Global Library, Ltd.
Printed and bound in China by CTPS

14 13 12 11
10 9 8 7 6 5 4 3 2 1

Library of Congress Cataloging-in-Publication Data
Gray, Susan Heinrichs.
   The life cycle of mammals / Susan H. Gray.
      p. cm.—(Life cycles)
   Includes bibliographical references and index.
   ISBN 978-1-4329-4981-5 (hc)—ISBN 978-1-4329-4988-4
(pb) 1. Mammals—Life cycles—Juvenile literature. I. Title.
   QL706.2.G732 2012
   599.156—dc22   2010038498

Acknowledgments
The author and publisher are grateful to the following for permission to reproduce copyright material: © Corbis: pp. 11 top (© Martin Harvey), 21 (© Joe McDonald), 24 (© W. Perry Conway), 33 (© JIM BOURG/Reuters); © Getty Images: p. 29 (National Geographic/Paul Nicklen); © iStockphoto: pp. 7 (© Ivan Kuzmin),14 (© Keith Szafranski), 41 (© Kjersti Joergensen); © Photolibrary: pp. 17 (Peter Arnold Images/ Doug Cheeseman), 19 (Superstock/Tom Brakefield), 20 (Age fotostock/Gerry Ellis), 23 (Peter Arnold Images/Mark Carwardine), 26 (First Light Associated Photographers/ Thomas Kitchin & Victoria Hurst), 45 (Peter Arnold Images RF); © Shutterstock: pp. 4 (© Uryadnikov Sergey), 5 top (© Krzysztof Odziomek), 5 bottom (© mlorenz), 8 (© John Carnemolla), 11 (© Shane White), 13 (© Peter Betts), 15 (© Jeff Grabert), 25 top (© nialat), 25 bottom (© Studiotouch), 27 (© markrhiggins), 28 (© Ivan Kuzmin), 30 (© Justin Black), 31 (© Naiyyer), 35 (© Alexander Lukin), 36 (© Riaan van den Berg), 37 (© Tihis), 38 (© Nestor Noci), 39 (© BlueOrange Studio).

Cover photograph of a giraffe reproduced with permission of © Corbis (© Torbjorn Arvidson/Nordicphotos).

We would like to thank Dr. Michael Bright for his invaluable help in the preparation of this book.

Every effort has been made to contact copyright holders of any material reproduced in this book. Any omissions will be rectified in subsequent printings if notice is given to the publisher.

Contents

Some words are shown in bold, **like this**. You can find out what they mean by looking in the glossary.

Look but don't touch: Many small mammals are easily hurt. If you see one in the wild, do not get too close to it. Look at it, but do not try to touch it!

What Is a Mammal?

A mammal is an animal that has hair. Almost all mammals give birth to live young. Only five **species**, or kinds, of mammals lay eggs. All female mammals produce milk to feed their babies.

Three groups

There are three main groups of mammals. One group is called the **monotremes**. These are the few mammals that lay eggs. The second group is made up of the **marsupials**. They give birth to very tiny babies. The babies make their way into their mother's pouch, where they continue to develop. The remaining mammals form the largest group—the **placental** mammals. They do not have pouches and therefore give birth to live young.

This mother shows some features that make her a mammal. She has hair on her body, and she produces milk to feed her baby.

Mammals are **vertebrates**. These are animals that have a backbone. Mammals are also warm-blooded creatures. This means that their body temperature always remains about the same. It does not cool down on cold days or heat up on warm days. Humans are mammals. So are pandas, house cats, dolphins, pigs, and giraffes, to name just a few.

Where's the Hair?

All mammals have hair. But it certainly is difficult to find on some animals such as the whale and the armadillo. Dolphins, whales, and **porpoises** do have hair, though. It appears as tiny bristles on their heads, snouts, or around their mouths. In some species, it falls out shortly after birth. Armadillos, on the other hand, have hair throughout their lives. It is coarse (rough) and grows on their bellies.

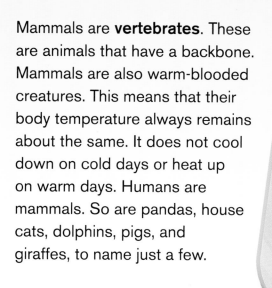

What Are the Different Kinds of Mammals?

There are about 5,000 **species** of mammals known today. Scientists believe that many mammals have not yet been discovered. Still, with 5,000 species, scientists need a method for sorting them out.

Scientists have organized the mammals by creating different groups and deciding which ones belong in which groups. The groups are based on similarities—ways in which the animals are alike. For instance, the **primate** group includes monkeys, gorillas, chimpanzees, and humans. The **canine** group includes dogs, wolves, and foxes.

Kingdom, phylum, and class

All mammals belong to one enormous group called the animal kingdom. Scientists divide the animal kingdom into smaller groups, and each one of these is called a **phylum**. In the animal kingdom, there is a phylum for flatworms, one for insects, crabs, and spiders, one for sea urchins and sand dollars, and so on. One phylum has the name **Chordata**. It includes animals that have a bundle of nerves, such as a spinal cord, running down their backs. Mammals, birds, fish, reptiles, and amphibians are members of the phylum Chordata.

Scientists further divide each phylum into classes. The class that includes all of the mammals is called **Mammalia**.

Where Do Bats Fit In?

In ancient times, people thought bats were types of birds. After all, both have wings and are good fliers. However, bats do not have feathers, as birds do. Their bodies are covered with short hairs. Also, bats do not lay eggs. They give birth to live, wriggling little bats. Today, bats are classified as mammals.

Smaller and smaller groups

Scientists divide the thousands of mammals into about 30 groups called orders. One order includes only elephants, one includes all the kinds of rabbits, one has only the armadillos, and so on. Orders are next divided into smaller groups called families. Families are divided into groups called **genera**. And each genus is divided into species. Every species is one particular kind of mammal.

Let's take a look at just one mammal and figure out which groups it belongs to. This is the dik-dik.

Here are a few of the groups in the animal kingdom. Where does the dik-dik fit in? Which phylum, class, and order does it belong to?

Animal Kingdom

Phylum Echinodermata (includes sea urchins and sand dollars)

Phylum Annelida (earthworms)

Phylum Arthropoda (includes insects and spiders)

Phylum Chordata (have a nerve bundle down their backs, usually as a spinal cord)

Class Amphibia (frogs, toads, and salamanders)

Class Reptilia (lizards, turtles, and other animals covered with scales or plates)

Class Aves (songbirds, owls, and others that have feathers and lay eggs)

Class Mammalia (animals with hair)

Order Diprotodontia (animals that have pouches where their young grow)

Order Rodentia (rats, squirrels, and other gnawing animals)

Order Artiodactyla (animals with two-toed hooves, such as giraffes, camels, and cattle)

Order Lagomorpha (includes hares and rabbits)

Order Cingulata (animals that have leathery armor on their bodies)

New Discoveries of Old Animals

Sometimes scientists discover bones of animals that became **extinct** long ago. They still classify these animals, though. If a newly discovered animal is similar to a living animal, it might be placed with it in the same phylum, class, order, family, or genus. If the new animal is totally unique, then scientists will create new groups for it.

How Is a Mammal Born?

Almost all mammals give birth to live young. The babies develop and grow inside the bodies of their mothers. When they are born, many look very much like their parents. For them, it is obvious that the babies and parents belong to the same **species**.

Different plans

Marsupials, however, do not fit this pattern. Their development begins inside their mothers, but they are still very tiny when they are born.

After birth, they creep along the outside of their mother's body, slowly making their way to a pouch on her belly. Once inside the pouch, they latch on to a nipple and begin to drink their mother's milk. Some marsupials spend weeks in the pouch, and others spend months, slowly growing and developing. Kangaroos are marsupials that are tiny, pink, and helpless at birth. After several months in the pouch, they look completely different.

The **monotremes** follow an entirely different plan. They lay eggs. Once the young hatch, they remain close to their mothers. The mothers produce milk from openings on their bodies. The milk leaks out onto their fur, where the babies lick it off. There are only a few monotreme species, and they all live in Australia and New Guinea (see page 11).

Egg Layers

The monotremes include the duckbill **platypus** (top) and several species of **echidna** or spiny anteater (bottom). They are found in Australia and New Guinea. The female platypus lays one or two eggs, while the echidna lays only one. Eggs hatch in about 10 days, and the babies of both animals are no bigger than jelly beans.

Dependent babies

Some mammal babies are completely helpless when they are born. Of course, tiny marsupial babies could never survive on their own. But many other mammals also start life small and weak. Puppies and kittens are born with their eyes closed. Their little legs are weak, and they can only squirm around. Hamsters are born with no fur, so they must stay close to their mothers for warmth.

These helpless babies depend completely on their parents for food and safety. But some stay with their parents long after they have grown strong. Tiger cubs, for example, will stay with their mother for months, learning how to hunt.

Ready to go

Many grazing animals have babies that are not so helpless. Within hours of birth, little horses, zebras, buffalo, and sheep are standing and walking around. Their spindly legs are almost as long as those of their parents. These babies are ready to get moving shortly after birth. This helps them survive. They are able to travel in the safety of a herd from the very start.

Got Hair?

Rabbits and hares are in the same order and they certainly look alike, so are there any differences between them? Yes! One difference is the amount of fur they have at birth. Rabbits are born without fur, while hares are covered with it. You might say that hares have hair!

Shortly after birth,
a baby giraffe begins
to learn to walk.

How Does a Mammal Grow?

All mammal babies start life on a diet of milk. This is the perfect food for them. It is easy to swallow, and they don't have to chew it up. Whales produce milk that is very rich and fatty. It is ideal for large newborns that live in cold water and need lots of nourishment. The milk of harp seals is loaded with fat and protein. These are exactly what the baby seals need. Drinking this rich milk helps them gain almost 2.3 kilograms (5 pounds) a day!

Carnivores

In time, babies begin to feed on other things. Some develop a taste for meat. These are the **carnivores**. Carnivores such as foxes and jaguars begin hunting small **prey** when they are young. In time, they also develop claws for catching their food, and sharp teeth for tearing it.

The wolf is clearly a meat eater. Its long sharp teeth are for piercing flesh.

Herbivores

Plant-eating mammals are called **herbivores**. An herbivore baby develops flattened teeth in the back of its mouth. Such teeth are perfect for grinding grass, leaves, and stems. Herbivores also develop long **digestive** systems. They need them to break down those tough plant materials. In horses, for example, the digestive system is more than 30 meters (100 feet) long!

Omnivores

Some babies belong to **species** that eat just about anything. These mammals are called **omnivores**, and they are not picky. They will eat insects, fruit, eggs, frogs, and fish.

This little raccoon is an omnivore. It might grow up to find and eat insects, fish, frogs, lizards, and even food left out for pets!

Living alone or with others

As mammals grow, they take on the habits and behaviors of their parents. In time, some strike out on their own. Others become part of flocks, herds, packs, **pods**, or colonies.

Virginia opossums, woodchucks, and skunks prefer to live **solitary** lives. Except when mothers are tending their young, these animals live alone. Big cats such as cougars and cheetahs keep their babies nearby for months. During this time, the young will chase one another, play, and wrestle. This is preparing them for life on their own, when they will have to chase and bring down prey.

Mammals that live in groups are called social animals. Group life has many advantages. Young that grow up living in a herd find safety among the many adults. They may also find other "mothers" willing to look out for them. Female howler monkeys, for example, sometimes adopt young monkeys who have lost their mothers.

Safety in Numbers

One good thing about living in a herd is that other members offer protection. When musk oxen of the Arctic feel threatened, the adults form a circle. They keep the young and weak oxen in the center of the ring. The adults face outward, ready to take on any attacker. This works great for the animals. Not many **predators** want to take on that angry bunch!

This mother is taking her cubs out hunting. At first, the young might actually be afraid of prey. But eventually, they sharpen their hunting skills.

How Do Mammals Move?

Mammals move in all kinds of ways. After all, they must travel on the ground, underwater, through trees, in pitch-black caves, and down in burrows. They each have ways to get around in these natural surroundings.

Mammals that spend part of their life underground are built for burrowing. They have strong arms and claws for digging in the dirt. Gophers and moles are excellent burrowers. They have tiny eyes and short hair that does not become matted with soil.

kangaroo

Here are just two of the mammals that are good jumpers. What do they have in common that makes them suited for this means of travel?

kangaroo rat

Herding animals have hooves that can withstand many hours of standing, walking, and running. The hooves are made of hard material that constantly grows as it is worn down. Most herding animals are not fierce fighters. However, they do have ways to escape their enemies. When alarmed, springboks and gazelles of Africa will leap high into the air, then land on all four feet. This spring-loaded method of travel is an excellent way to surprise and outdistance **predators**.

This little **kinkajou** spends most of its time high in the trees of South America. Notice its large, clawed hands, which are good for clinging to branches. The kinkajou can turn its feet backward. This allows it to run forward or backward along a tree trunk or branch. It can also hang from tree limbs by its long tail.

Other ways to travel

Tree-dwelling mammals get around by leaping, swinging, and gliding. Many **primates** live in trees. Some have small, slender, athletic bodies and strong arms and legs. They can quickly scamper up a tree trunk and leap nimbly from limb to limb. Examples are the squirrel monkeys and spider monkeys. Gibbons are primates with incredibly long arms, hands, and fingers. They swing from tree to tree, often sailing through the air to grab the next branch.

Made for the water

Some mammals are built for **aquatic** travel. The otter and the **platypus** are not closely related, but they both spend much of their time in the water. They have webbed feet for swimming and muscular tails for steering.

This gibbon knows how to get around. Its fingers are naturally curved into a hook shape. How might this help the gibbon as it travels from branch to branch?

Many mammals spend all of their time in water. These include whales, dolphins, and **porpoises**. Rather than having arms, legs, paws, hooves, and tails, they have fins, flippers, and **flukes**. These structures help to propel (move) them to great depths and back to the surface where they can breathe. Their streamlined bodies can easily shoot through the water, and their large stores of fat provide energy for swimming.

Look at Me!

Like a flying squirrel, this sugar glider does not fly, but actually sails through the air. It has large, thin skin flaps along its sides and stretching between its hands and feet. These flaps work like a parachute to help the animal glide from tree to tree.

Migrations

Some mammals spend their entire lives within a small area. Little mammals, such as shrews, may stay within a small section of a field for their entire lives. Other, larger mammals, such as the rhinoceros, might travel within an area the size of a small town. But the greatest travelers of all are those that make long trips every year called **migrations**.

Mammals that make these trips are doing it to survive. They migrate in order to find food for themselves and for their young. Reindeer and gray whales are two examples of migrating mammals.

Reindeer, or caribou, live in northern Europe, Asia, and North America. They feed on spongy plantlike foods called **lichens**. As the weather cools in the fall, the northernmost lichens begin disappearing and the reindeer head south. Their migrations take them several hundred miles to where food is plentiful. When warmer weather returns, the reindeer trek north again. With an abundance of fresh lichens available, they can continue feeding and have their calves.

Up and Down

Not all migrations are long, difficult trips. Dall sheep in Alaska simply migrate up and down the mountainsides. They spend their summers in the mountaintops, then move to the valleys in the wintertime. In the lower areas, there is less snow and food is easier to find.

This gray whale is making its annual migration. Gray whales often leap out of the water and fall back with a splash. Scientists are not sure why the whales do this.

A long swim

In the summer months, gray whales live in the northern Pacific Ocean, along the coastlines of North America and Russia. Because of the long, sunny summer days, the waters are packed with life, and the whales find plenty to eat. As winter approaches, the whales head south. They have their young in the warm waters near Mexico and Korea, and remain for another two to three months before returning north. These whales travel more than 16,000 kilometers (10,000 miles) each year.

How Do Mammals Protect Themselves?

Some mammals actively protect themselves. They may hide, run, or fight. Others find safety in just being themselves. These animals depend on their natural size, colors, and habits for protection.

Killer whales and grizzly bears are enormous mammals. Few animals are likely to threaten them. But not all mammals have the advantage of size. Smaller mammals such as fennecs in the African desert count on their color to protect them. Fennecs are small sand-colored foxes that blend in perfectly with their environment.

This badger, found in Minnesota, protects itself in two ways. It is **nocturnal** and it hides out in a burrow.

Mammals that create burrows have natural hiding places. Chipmunks build very complex burrows. They include tunnels and separate "rooms" for sleeping, caring for babies, and storing food. The tunnels have well-hidden entrance holes and may run 9 meters (30 feet) long, providing excellent hiding places.

Many mammals prefer to be active at night. These nocturnal animals escape not only the heat of the day, but also the daytime **predators**. Bats are the ultimate nocturnal animals. By having the ability to fly, by feeding only at night, and by retreating to caves and other sheltered places in the day, they escape many different threats.

Snowshoe hares live in Canada and the northern United States. In the winter, their coats are almost solid white. In the summer, new fur grows in that is brown and gray in color. How do these winter and summer colors protect the animal from predators?

Great escapes

When many mammals feel threatened, they fight, run, roll up in a ball, or use other ways to protect themselves. Fighting mammals such as bears, wolves, and lions use their claws and teeth to deal with threats. Sometimes they even do battle with members of their own **species** to protect their young or defend their homes.

Herding animals usually just run from danger. However, this does not mean they are defenseless. Zebras can kick a predator senseless. And musk oxen can trample an enemy to death.

Skunks are gentle animals, but they do have one powerful weapon—their spray. When a skunk senses danger, it lowers its head, arches its back, and stamps its feet. If that doesn't scare an enemy away, the skunk lifts its tail and sprays a foul-smelling fluid.

Meerkats watch out for danger while other family members look for food. When they see danger, they make high-pitched sounds.

Certain small animals that live in colonies have ways of protecting the whole group. Some prairie dogs and meerkats station themselves as guards while the rest of the colony eats. When danger threatens, the guards bark out a warning and all of the members shoot for their burrows.

A few mammals defend themselves in very quiet ways. The Virginia opossum keels over and plays dead. Predators lose interest in the animal and leave it alone. The **pangolin** of Africa is covered in scales. When threatened, this toothless animal curls up into a tight ball and waits for the danger to pass.

Where Do Mammals Live?

Mammals live in just about every place imaginable, from the equator to the Arctic. Small mammals live underground. Climbing and swinging mammals live in trees. Other mammals live in grasslands, forests, deserts, swamps, and caves.

Mammals such as walruses and seals that are built for icy cold regions have certain things in common. They have thick layers of fat for **insulation**. The mothers also produce very rich milk for their young. It helps them to gain weight quickly and add to their own insulation.

Those mammals that live in hot, dry areas are also **adapted** for their environments. The tiny, mouse-like elephant shrew of Africa has tan fur that blends with its surroundings. Although water is in short supply, the shrew gets all of the fluid it needs from eating ants, termites, and plants.

This four-toed elephant shrew lives in Kenya.

A Deep-Sea Diver

The narwhal is a whale that lives in the frigid waters of the Arctic. It is known to dive as deep as 1,372 meters (4,500 feet) and to remain underwater for almost 30 minutes. The animal's rib cage is flexible and collapses somewhat as the whale descends. During long stretches underwater, the narwhal shuts off its blood flow to certain organs. This is how it uses oxygen. By doing this, the whale does not have to return quickly to the surface to breathe.

A problem up high

Mammals that live high in the mountains face one big problem. There is not much oxygen available in the air. People who climb mountains often face this "thin air." They find themselves gasping for breath. But llamas can be found high in the mountains of South America, and deer mice can live up in the mountains of North America. Why aren't they gasping for air?

This llama is built for life in the mountains. It is sure-footed and can walk on rocky ground. Its coat protects it from the cold. And its blood cells easily take up oxygen.

The camel has several adaptations to protect it from wind and sand storms. The long eyelashes protect the eyes. The nostrils can clamp shut to keep out the blowing sand.

It's in their blood

The blood cells of llamas and deer mice are a little different from those of other mammals. When mammals breathe in, oxygen enters their lungs. It next moves into the blood cells that are traveling in vessels through their lungs. The blood cells carry oxygen out to all of the body's tissues. In llamas and deer mice, the blood cells pick up oxygen much more easily than in other mammals. These animals do not gasp for oxygen. Their body tissues get plenty of it.

No matter where mammals live, they have adaptations that help them survive. Some mammals, such as the house mouse and the brown rat, have adapted to just about every environment. Today, they live almost everywhere on Earth.

How Do Mammals Help Us?

Mammals are important in nature and also helpful to humans. All mammals are **consumers**. This means they eat, or consume, plants and other animals. This helps keep balance in nature. For example, little brown bats eat thousands of mosquitoes each night. Thanks to this bat, the mosquito population does not grow out of control.

Many mammals become food items for other mammals. Foxes eat mice, for instance, and polar bears eat seals. Those mammals that have no natural enemies are called the apex **predators**. They are large meat eaters that do not become **prey** for other animals.

This simple food web shows how mammals depend on plants and other animals for their food. The mouse eats grain and insects. Snakes, hawks, and foxes eat mice. Hawks eat snakes. Here, hawks and foxes are at the top of the web, as no other animals eat them.

hawk

fox

snake

mice

insect

grain

Humans often use cattle, deer, and many other mammals for their meat. People also drink goat, cow, and yak milk, or use it to make cream, cheese, and yogurt. People use fur and leather made from animal skins for clothing. And many people rely on elephants and camels to carry loads, oxen to pull heavy wagons, and horses and donkeys for transportation.

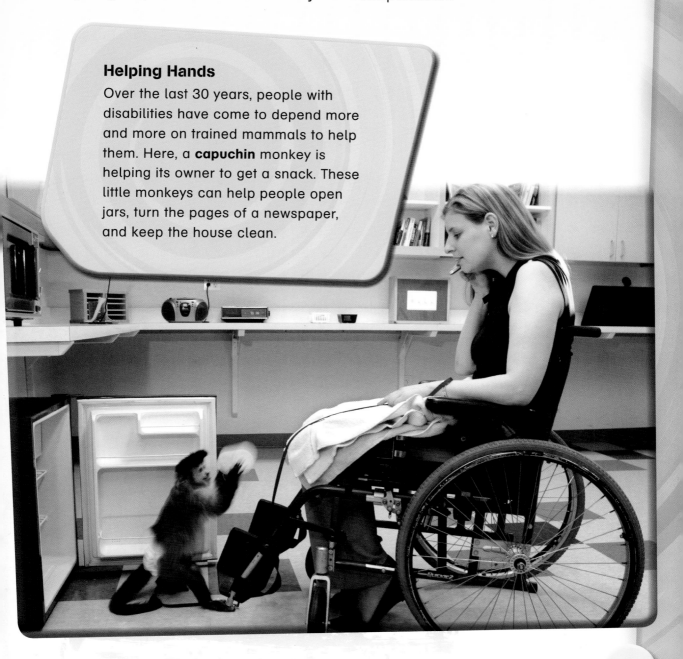

Helping Hands

Over the last 30 years, people with disabilities have come to depend more and more on trained mammals to help them. Here, a **capuchin** monkey is helping its owner to get a snack. These little monkeys can help people open jars, turn the pages of a newspaper, and keep the house clean.

Problems from mammals

In some cases, mammals have caused problems. But this is not always their fault. When people move into new areas, they sometimes destroy mammal habitats. They fill in ponds and cut trees to make room for homes. They may not know they are destroying the mammals' food supply. But this may cause coyotes or mountain lions to come into town looking for prey. It may force wolves to attack sheep or cattle.

Mammals that are **invasive species** create immense problems. Invasive animals are those that are brought into new environments and begin to take over. They may have no natural enemies, so their numbers quickly increase. In Australia and New Zealand, the European wild rabbit is an invasive species. It was brought to these lands in the 1800s and spread quickly. The rabbit eats crop plants, grass, roots, seeds, leaves, and even bark. Experts are now trying different ways to remove these pests.

Some mammals can carry and spread disease. For instance, squirrels, prairie dogs, chipmunks, rats, and mice carry a germ that causes **plague**. The germ can spread to humans and cause fever, chills, and even death. Throughout history, the disease has wiped out millions of people. Fortunately, we now have ways to detect and treat the disease.

A Foreign Invader

The American mink is an invasive species in the British Isles. It was imported to be raised for its fur. However, some minks escaped, and their population grew in the wild. The American mink feeds on the water vole, a small ratlike mammal. Now, the vole's numbers have greatly decreased.

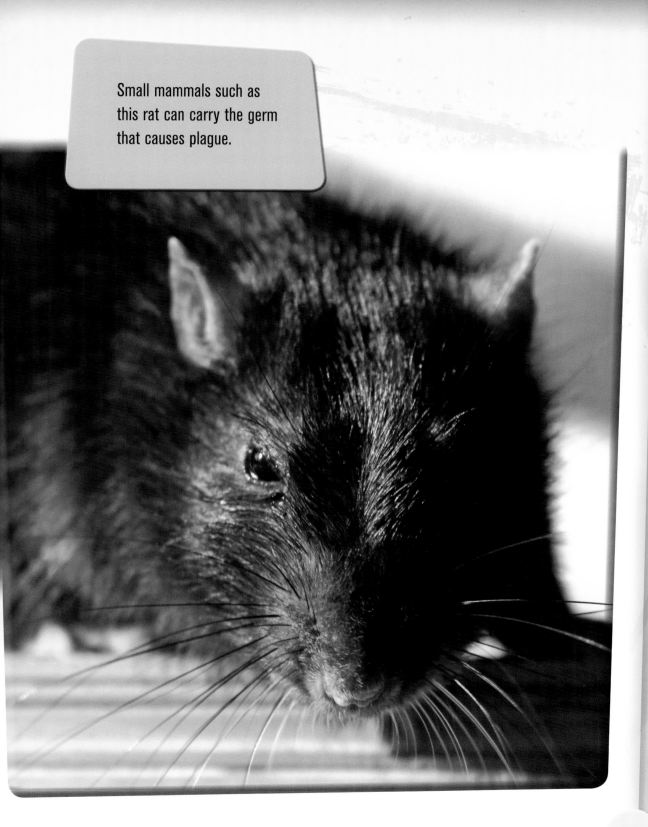

Small mammals such as this rat can carry the germ that causes plague.

How Do Mammals Spend Their Time?

Mammals spend much of their time resting and sleeping. At rest, a mammal's breathing and heart rate slow down. Larger mammals such as elephants and hippopotamuses already have slow breathing and heart rates. An elephant's heart beats only about 30 times each minute. Very small mammals such as guinea pigs and gerbils have much faster rates. Either way, these processes speed up when the animals are active and slow down when they are not.

Tiny mammals such as this shrew live life in the fast lane. These animals eat constantly. They have a heart rate of about 15 beats per second, and they take more than 700 breaths each minute.

Some mammals really know how to slow things down—they hibernate. During hibernation, the body processes slow down to almost a dead stop. Bats, woodchucks, and ground squirrels are examples of hibernating animals. Before the cold weather comes, these animals eat constantly to build up their fat. They also find a den or burrow where they can hibernate. Once they slide into a hibernating state, they appear to be dead. Different **species** hibernate for different lengths of time, some for weeks and some for months. But when warm weather returns, they rouse themselves and become active again.

Hedgehogs in Hibernation
Hedgehogs are animals that hibernate each winter. During hibernation, this animal's heart rate slows from 190 beats to 20 beats per minute. Its body temperature drops to almost the freezing point.

Other things to do

When mammals aren't resting, they are usually busy looking for food, eating, or caring for their families. **Diurnal** mammals are animals that are active mainly during the day. They often have fur that blends in with their environment. This way, they can move about in the daytime and still be protected from their enemies.

Yum!

The giant anteater has arms, hands, and a head built for finding food. It uses its claws to make a hole in a termite mound or anthill. Next, it pokes its snout straight into the hole. Then the anteater flicks its long tongue back and forth, in and out, picking up the tiny insects and pulling them into its mouth. An adult anteater can slurp up more than 30,000 ants and termites a day!

Nocturnal mammals are busy at night. Some have unusually large eyes that help them see in the dark. But others, such as some bats, are different.

The insect-eating bats do not use their eyesight to find food in the dark. They use sound waves instead. As the bat flies about, it sends out sound waves. The waves hit other objects in the area and bounce back to the bat. The bat's brain interprets those returning waves, so the bat knows which objects are still and which ones are moving. The bat can even tell how fast insects are flying and their direction. This method of finding food is called **echolocation**.

This little tarsier is a nocturnal animal. Its huge eyes help it find food and spot **predators** in the dark.

How Do Mammals Have Babies?

Some mammals can have babies at any time of the year. They do not need to wait for a particular season that is best for bearing young. Humans are the perfect example of this. Other mammals, however, need to wait until food and water become plentiful. At that time, their young have the best chance of survival.

Before babies are born, the parents must choose each other as mates. In some mammals, chemicals help them make this choice. Many animals produce chemicals that are signals to other members of their **species**. In dogs, females produce these chemicals when they are ready to mate. Male dogs sense the chemicals, even from far away.

Courtship

Other mammals use courtship activities to attract mates. Male humpback whales seem to "sing" to females, for up to 30 minutes, hoping to get their attention. Male Tasmanian devils are less delicate. During courtship, the males and females snarl and wrestle with each other before mating.

Sometimes males must run off their competition before attracting a female. The males of bighorn sheep butt heads to determine which ones will get to mate. Sometimes this will go on for hours. The more powerful sheep win the females. The weaker sheep might have to wait a whole year before they compete again, perhaps with better luck.

A Nosey Monkey

Proboscis monkeys live in trees on the large island of Borneo (located north of Australia). The male monkeys have huge noses that can reach a length of 18 centimeters (7 inches). Each time the male makes his *kee-honk* sound, the nose straightens out. Some scientists believe they might do this to attract females.

Time before birth

After mating, the young mammals grow or form within eggs in the bodies of their mothers. The length of time before birth is called the gestation period. It is different for different species. Babies of the Virginia opossum grow for only 12 days before they are born and crawl into their mother's pouch. Asian elephants have a much longer gestation period. It takes about 22 months before their babies are ready for birth.

Cycle of life

Once the babies are born, the life cycle begins again. The young grow up and learn to find food and shelter for themselves. Some die before they start families of their own. They cannot find food, are eaten by **predators**, or they become ill. If they survive, they find mates and have young of their own. Some mammals, such as field mice, lead busy, short lives. Other mammals, such as whales, may live into their forties and beyond. As long as the cycle continues, the species will survive.

Becoming Parents

Large animals are usually much older than small ones when they are ready to have babies. Rats can give birth when they are only three months old. Hippopotamuses begin having babies when they are eight or nine years of age.

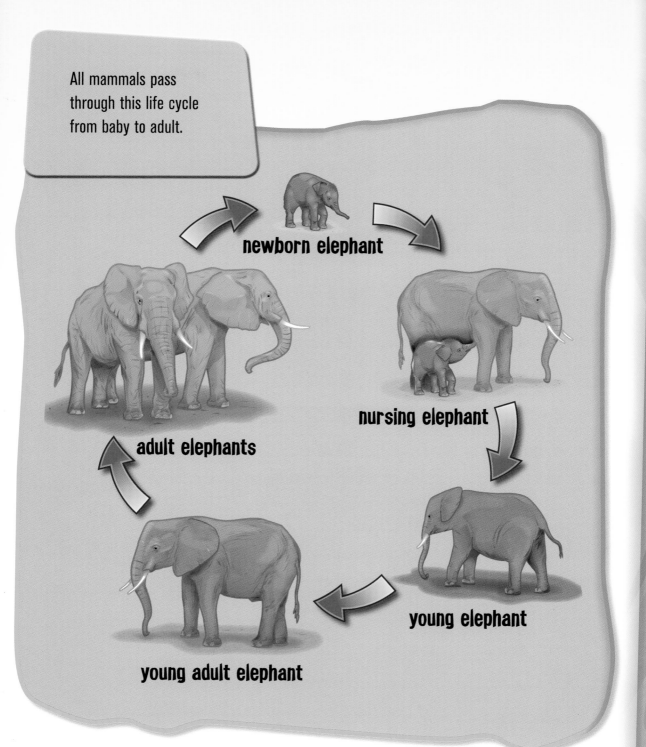

All mammals pass through this life cycle from baby to adult.

newborn elephant

nursing elephant

adult elephants

young elephant

young adult elephant

Mammal Facts

What is the largest living mammal?

The African elephant is the largest land mammal. But at 30 meters (100 feet) in length, the blue whale is the largest of all living things. The whale's tongue alone weighs as much as an elephant!

What is the smallest living mammal?

The bumblebee bat of Thailand is the smallest mammal. It measures only 32 millimeters (1.3 inches) in length.

What is the fastest mammal?

The cheetah is the fastest land mammal. It can run at speeds of up to 113 kilometers per hour (70 miles per hour), but only for short bursts.

What is the loudest land mammal?

The howler monkey is the winner here. The cries of the male can reach other monkeys about 5 kilometers (3 miles) away!

Mammal classification

Scientists divide the 5,000 or so mammals into about 30 different orders. About 2,000 species are in the order of rats, mice, squirrels, and other **rodents**. Another 1,000 are included in the order of bats. All other orders are much smaller. They include the order of shrews and moles, and the order of **carnivores** such as jaguars, hyenas, and bears. The order of **primates** has about 300 **species** and includes humans, apes, and monkeys. The **platypus** and the aardvark each fit into an order of their own.

The aardvark is all alone in its order. This African mammal is **nocturnal** and eats termites. An adult weighs more than a large dog.

Glossary

adapt to adjust to new or different conditions

aquatic living in or near water, or dealing with water

canine belonging to the group of doglike animals

capuchin type of monkey

carnivore animal that eats other animals

Chordata phylum of animals that have a cord of nerve tissue down their backs at some time in their lives

consumer living thing that eats plants or animals

digestive having to do with digestion or breaking down food

diurnal active mainly during the daytime

echidna small, spiny monotreme of Australia

echolocation method of detecting things by bouncing sound waves off them

extinct having died out

fluke finlike part of a whale's tail

genus (pl. genera) classification level of the animal kingdom

herbivore animal that eats plants

insulation covering or layer for keeping something warm

invasive referring to something that intrudes or pushes its way in

kinkajou tree-living mammal with a long tail

lichen plantlike organism composed of a fungus and an alga living together

Mammalia class of animals that have hair and produce milk for their young

marsupial pouched mammal that gives birth to very small young, that then grow and develop in the pouch

migration trip made by animals, usually every year

monotreme mammal that lays eggs

nocturnal active mainly at night

omnivore animal that eats both plant and animal tissues

pangolin insect-eating mammal whose body is covered by scales

phylum one of the major groups within the animal kingdom

plague disease that causes death and spread quickly to a large number of people

placental referring to mammals that do not have a pouch and that give birth to live young

platypus Australian mammal with a duck-like bill and that lays eggs

pods small group of animals traveling together

porpoise aquatic animal similar to the dolphin

predator animal that kills another animal for food

prey animal that is eaten by other animals

primate mammal group consisting of humans, apes, and monkeys

proboscis unusually long snout

rodent animal with two large upper front teeth for gnawing.

solitary living or doing things alone

species particular kind of living thing

vertebrate animal with a backbone

Find Out More

Books

Bishop, Nic. *Marsupials*. New York: Scholastic, 2009.

Green, Jen. *Mammal*. New York: DK Children, 2005.

Kalman, Bobbie. *What Is a Carnivore?* New York: Crabree, 2009.

Rhodes, Mary Jo, and David Hall. *Dolphins, Seals, and Other Sea Mammals*. New York: Children's Press, 2007.

Websites

Environmental Education for Kids: Hibernation
http://dnr.wi.gov/org/caer/ce/eek/nature/snugsnow.htm

National Geographic Kids: Creature Features
http://kids.nationalgeographic.com/kids/animals/creaturefeature

Smithsonian National Zoological Park: Small Mammals
http://nationalzoo.si.edu/Animals/SmallMammals/ForKids/default.cfm

Index